Love Letter to the Young'uns

Be Prepared

by

Shirley M. Hearne-Clark

DORRANCE
PUBLISHING CO
EST. 1920
PITTSBURGH, PENNSYLVANIA 15238

Dorrance Publishing Co
585 Alpha Drive
Pittsburgh, PA 15238
Visit our website at *www.dorrancebookstore.com*

ISBN: 979-8-89027-013-9
eISBN: 979-8-89027-511-0

Dedicated to the Hearne Five

Johnie, Fannie, Pernitha, and Brenda La Faye,

my loving husband Camille G. Clark

My team of encouragers, who love(d) me unconditionally,

My daughters Enijua Johara, Elizabeth Faine,

Whom I love unconditionally,

and the entire Patterson and Hearne Clans

(you already know)

CONTENTS

INTRODUCTION

My life and the aging process are the factors that contributed to my commitment to writing this book and its completion to a reality. The aging process had plagued me for years. However, when I turned the age of sixty-five, I realized I was not prepared for the process. I thought of my daughter and generations that would be as unprepared. I started speaking out about authoring a book about aging to younger people as I complained about my personal story of difficulties. For example the young man who gave me a jump for my car battery, or the young women at the store, to anyone who would listen. I desired to catch their reaction, most agreed it would be a clever idea, seniors were all in. Most found it amusing that was just the push I needed! I was in school obtaining a couple of degrees as I authored the chapters created. I would write, stop, change my mind, and begin again. After completing school, I decided to sit myself down and begin writing. I am in the middle of my seventy-second life chapter and I am finishing, prayerfully publishing before turning seventy-three. I am aging all through this book. I wrote this introduction as I began final corrections and awaiting the artwork. I hope it is enjoyed, aging is better when you are not alone and understand the ins and outs!

CHAPTER 1
Who I am, What I Believe, & Purpose

As a believer, I understand that I am a spirit, I have a soul that lives in a created body. (1 Thessalonians 5:23). The word of God says, God will care for us always, "even to hair white with age" (Isaiah 46:4). My mind and memory are "blessed" according to Proverbs 10:7. For me, knowing this is important concerning the process of aging and its preparedness. No one provided information regarding aging or mindfulness as to how it is accomplished and how to maintain and survive. Sure, there were articles and books giving insight into what to and not to eat, exercise, keep moving, rest, I needed something a little more personal. I begin to recognize that little by little my body and its functions would overload, and eventually crash! That crash came in the form of a conversation and a realization I had with myself, "I'm old!" Watching my body go south, and laziness settle in comfortably is something you slip into without fanfare or special attention. Personally, I am rolling with it (sort of) and doing the best I can.

I am not saying this is everyone's story but, it is mine. I am sharing and believe there may be other sixty to seventy plus year old ladies and men, raised in South Central LA, or any part of this globally connected world (pandemic proven). I know there are some who had to steer themselves through the aging process without a clue at the aging onset! Noticeable aging began for me at forty-five. The changes were slight, but I was aware something was up, I shrugged it off. The next five years, well, let us say the aging process was unavoidable; it *was* happening! I was about to enter the twilight zone of senior Dom! I will attempt to give you an example. Life changes started as a young girl I went to sleep with no breasts and woke up with only *one* growing! (My mother refused to buy a bra for one breast). The aging mirror has the same shock value, you go to sleep remembering and wake up cannot remember much of anything until the first cup of coffee or tea, even after that memory is a toss up! Please, never tell another *golden* (senior) to remind you of this or that it will be void of memory status; it is just forgotten! The realization that you are aging takes on another level of meaning as people start referring to you as *ma'am, mother, mama, those* from the Hispanic and Asian cultures call you *Mommie.* Older men folk are referred to as *pops, papa, senior, or elder*! These are mind-bending effects when other folks begin to recognize that you are aging. Can someone say "checkmate"? It is official, everyone knows!

My best friend Edna (God rest her soul) said a young women recognized her with, "Mother, let me get that door for you."

She wanted to push her down and step over her. Instead, she faked a smile said, "Thank you baby!"

It is hard to accept aging until one day you realize that this is your new life, I am here, and I will make the best of it. I began to reckon with the fact that the alternatives to aging are living unaware, cared for in a senior facility, or the infamous dirt nap before eternal life. Those facts of reality keep me in a state of gratefulness and living each day hopeful and joyful. At the onset of this writing, I was beginning another life chapter, overweight, and cautious about both my physical and mental health status. I walk occasionally, have a treadmill in my bedroom, and I am still active with minimal pain. I am thankful to God to still be among the living with a reasonable mind and joy in life!

For those who think I should have taken up body building to stay firm, had a face lift, or joined a gym, I believe in growing old with grace, being an example to others. That is my story, and I am sticking to it. I am *growing old gracefully*! I authored this book for the *young'uns* to encourage them to keep living, not to stumble into senior life as I did. This book is written for those who will live to grow old and enjoy it. There are advantages to sticking around. You begin to appreciate life and garner a new perspective of people, embrace a global attitude, and take life a step, and a day, at a time. My daughter, nieces, or young friends say, "You are getting old." My standard comeback, "keep living." Prayerfully, they will grow old. This book is meant to be a funny look at aging. I will use a few quotes or stats, a few scriptures that help drive home a point. I will toss in names of my family and friends because they are a part of my life, and it is part of the sharing. I hope to write again. I want you to know my folk. I am sharing my journey in the hope that it will help someone regarding the life changes, and surprises accompanying aging so that you will find grace in a time of need (Hebrews 4:16) and produce a welcoming mind-set. The gratitude for the process of aging, elevated wisdom, and spiritual fortitude is a great beginning. The key for me has been an open and strong relationship with God. However, there are added services that I enjoy. I get free *looked-after* services from strangers I meet; they listen to my spontaneous conversations when I am out and about, doors are held open, things are picked up when dropped. I am grateful to God, for those who have touched my life, and the lives I have touched. Secondly, the appreciation for the things in life that are constant and things new and surprising. Thirdly, an ability to laugh at things that once stirred me up, and to cry for unimportant things that touch my heart and do both openly. Fourth, love unmeasured for family, friends, and the things in this physical realm created just for us by God. The ability to know life is a journey to growth and finding purpose! To understand people are created as image bearers by God and have access to all things good and the ability to come through those things that challenge us. Life is full of changes, and for me slowing down was hard, especially from those things that I enjoy. Spending time with others, assisting in any way I can, or making memories with those I love. In my younger life, I was a busy bee with committees, church, and community events. I could not get enough! I had to slow myself down, and learn to say no. I love my life, I love people, especially the people of God. No one is perfect. I love the fact that those who are believers strive to be at their best, and sometimes be the difference in the lives of others. Do Christians have life warts? Indeed, we do, perfection is what is strived for not always reached. It is the effort that sets the believer apart, the effort to *become (thanks Michelle Obama*)* the created by the Creator. I pray young'uns that you receive an understanding about aging that will help you through your personal aging journey. Seniors/elders I hope you get a chuckle from the reality you are experiencing. ENJOY!

CHAPTER 2
I Did it Right?

Every decade we all try to accomplish goals, change perspectives, improve our cognitive processes, adjust priorities, grow ethically, morally, spiritually, and personalized our views for the good, hopefully. I pray these are facts for every age or decade of our lives. The physical changes to your body practically go without notice between the ages of twenty to forty unless, there are physical or mental health challenges. To those who have physical or mental challenges, prayers for your healing and that love surrounds you to help you heal. Hoping also there is someone to help you journey through the process. To everyone there is humor in this little book, embrace it. Life occurrences are often better understood in someone else's shoes. So, I am allowing my personal story of aging to provide you with the gift of laughter and a journey being traveled. Physical changes in my body had to be acknowledge seriously at fifty. I noticed that my body was not as *perky* as I thought, heading downward fast. I began to sag and not in my pants, but my entire body! Well, I thought the answer to be exercise, eating healthy food, to rest more, drink water and, those foods that brought me joy I tried to stay away from. I did it right? There was just one problem, my adrenaline rush to keep this up fell short after three months my eating habits did change with cheating every now and then.

Keep this in mind, that from the ages of fifty-one to fifty-nine each year brings change, bodily or mentally, related to aging. It ranges from hair loss to a runny nose, your knees, joint noise, or dry skin, accommodating changes in sleeping positions to prevent painful shoulders or hips. Hopefully, knowing the pitfalls of aging will help you cope or *do it right* when it is expected. There are those who can relate to my journey. I would hate to think I am alone with these issues! We should all learn to look for the lessons, love life, enjoy at any age, and listen to our body, it will tell the story! Living in this microwave society (quick fix) has been confusing for me, how about you? We often ignore or pay little or no attention to things that would help us age with grace and comfort, such as preparing our finances, physical and mental health checks, spiritual life, adjustments to our moral/ethical attitudes. Let me drop a word that I found helpful during this process "contentment" being happy or satisfied, at any age we should seek it out, you will thank me for that one!

I was raised in a church family, my cultural roots and family traditions dictated my values, prevented me from going too far down the rabbit hole of trouble or danger. Peer pressure for my sisters and I was minimal. The stopgate was named Ms. Fannie my mother, five feet two-inch-tall, old-school, scary when there was a need to be! Not that we were perfect kids, but we did not go looking for problems that would put us before her negatively. My dad Johnie was a #girldad before that saying was coined, (thank you Kobe Bryant). He protected, followed, and carried us everywhere and picked us up from everywhere we wanted to go. School dances, house parties (where he stayed), football games, need I say more? Restrictions were worn as clothing for my sisters and me.

Substantial changes occurred for me between the ages sixty to sixty-nine; it was a trip! The years were speeding up, I turned sixty and then I was sixty-nine. There seemed only to be three months in the year, at this stage of aging January the new year, July (my birthday), and holy moly it is December! Each year in my sixties brought new body and mental revelations, my head was truly spinning. To add to this fast-moving movie, I got married in 2016 just before I turned sixty-six. My husband Camille is a sweet, loving, kind man who adores me and I adore him. Baby, when you have been single for thirty plus years it is work to re-marry as a senior. Sorry, I digressed, that is a subject for another book. Please know my husband and I work together and we are building a covenant supportive aging marriage.

To *get it right* you must come to an understanding about aging it will happen with or without your say or understanding! People have unusual ways to accomplish the coping aspect. Group 1 (not going to age) will try everything on the market that says it will prevent, change, or slow down the aging process. Creams and elixirs, foods eaten, or clothes worn, they will attempt to snap that body back in place. The truth is heredity is in charge along with your mental attitude. Next time you are at a family gathering, look around. Heredity is staring you in the face! My sisters and I did not take notice the broad shoulders of Johnie (our dad), his oversized knees that my sister Brenda inherited, and receding hair or what some refer to as cowlick hair line (all three of us wear), or the oversized forehead, (thank you Dad) came as a surprise. The hands of Fannie (our mom), her compassion, warrior attitude when it came to family, her spiritual prowess, also were inherited along with our dad's patience. As we all grow older, we begin to appreciate the heredity, the looks, the wit, the ability to use wisdom when it matters. Heredity may throw you curves or fast balls, but you can now be prepared and embrace it. When you begin to step into the persona/heredity shoes of a loved one, it will give you pause, and a smile.

Group 2 - Oh well, bring it on let's get this party started! Group 3 - Fearful, sometimes with validity. They are alone, or in a facility that often does not offer compassion or programs that encourage this stage of life. It is good if a senior must be placed in a facility, family, and friend visits with consistency it is essential! Young'uns pay attention along way, take note of your life, enjoy, and plan. When you look up and aging is approaching you will not faint but run on and see what comes in life prayerfully, purposefully, and hopefully with no regret.

CHAPTER 3
Why is my Body not Listening?

Simple operational tasks my body performed only a brief time ago have diminished such as standing and balance. It is as if my body and I cannot reach an understanding, and it acts occasionally independent of my instructions. Does my body need a hearing-aid? Oh wait, I am already wearing two! I could once a brief time ago, from a sitting position stand up, and immediately accomplish a movement or the thing I set out to do. Now, I must have a conversation, first with my knees, then my legs.

"Come, let's reason together please. I am going to the restroom, and we cannot dilly dally."

I have learned to lean my body forward to promote a forward action, with momentum being the driving force with hope in my heart that I can complete the task. With my knees simi-locked, while my legs balance my weight, *hallelujah*, mission accomplished! My hands are not any better, the arthritis or the twins (old folk joke) chime in as a hinderance. My grip is not what it was, and the strength is seeping out it seems by the minute. I have learned leveraging, which means using other things to carry some things. The phalanges (fingers) appear to have become clumsy and thicker, using them to text messages by swiping on my phone is problematic the gliding process is now compromised. Often, my phone stops providing options to my thoughts and fingers, the cursor merely blinks and waits. I am guessing my smart phone has recognized my aging process. I found a way of managing; I now use the little microphone to dictate short text and do research. Voila, a solution!

Please understand growing old does not mean giving up, I stay in the fight. Hopefully, you too will develop alternatives, a unique way of completing tasks with humor. Aging brings about adjusting and doing things differently. Sometimes painfully, I figured it out and so will you. Thoughtfulness is not just for others, it is applicable towards yourself. Relax, it will all work out, some of the lessons are not easily learned. Let me give you a good example, waiting to the last minute to go to the restroom. Tragedy strikes enough that you get smart and go before there is a significant urge. I no longer get on my knees to look for things under *anything*, too hard to get up. I promise you the sound my knees made the first time I bent over, the crackle-pop was too much. I did not desire to hear it often. If it is too high to reach, I call my six-foot two-inch husband Camille, to reach it or coax the dogs to bring things to me or forget about it. I have what the doctor calls frozen shoulder, and contrary to what my mother believed, W-D 40 will not help the hinges/joints on your body! I can never find my glasses, keys, or phone. To my credit, I never play "Sherlock" when I cannot find things in my home I sit until the object finds me, usually by accident. I have refused to wear the chain with clips to keep up with my glasses (two pairs are lost in the house at this very moment). I cannot wear bi-focals, it affects my balance. So the solution is two pairs of glasses, one for seeing the other for reading. Like most, I am afraid to lose my phone, it is my lifeline, office, and confidant, it often requires a search party in my home, which makes me nuts!

I am not complaining about aging, I just was not prepared. Hopefully, I can provide the young'uns with a few solutions! Did you know there are apps and devices that can help you find things? Research them, this is a public announcement! No one schooled me that not keeping my body warm as a young'un during season change could one day be a problem for my body's health. Something to keep in mind while you can. Today, that decision to be cute and dress skimpy is biting me in my hip, shoulders, knees, ankles, and my *butt* (sciatica). When the seasons change, we must respect the elements (cold, rain, the chill factor). You should dress accordingly. There *is* a reason; learn young'uns or one day *you* will pay. Young'uns, when winter and fall arrive, try and keep your body warm. The sun is not the same in the winter, it does not supply the same warmth as in the summer.

Make it a habit to eat more vegetables than meat. If you turn vegan, just learn what proteins you can exchange for meats; do it properly. Our wonderful bodies have a limit on substitutions and what is required to stay healthy. Cooked veggies are great, I like eating what I call *live foods*, salads, cucumbers, tomatoes, and fruits. These are the things that will give you a healthy colon and keep things moving if you get my meaning. If you jog keep jogging, walk, ride a bike, or join a gym. It is good for the respiratory and circulatory system. Do what is best for you, stay away from stressful situations, always rest. I take naps just like a kid. I am not ashamed, and I am a better person to deal with after my nap! I understand when I rest, it rolls over to the benefit of those around me. My contacts or interactions are profoundly more peaceful when I get the appropriate amount of rest. We have all seen the actions of a young child who is fighting a nap. Well, imagine that challenge at twenty times to the thirtieth power for a senior who has words, and triple threat actions to work with and agitated due to not having a nap! Again, do what is best for you to remain calm, engaging, and stress free, it promotes openness, and good vibes when needed spiritually, physically, and mentally. David wrote, "my flesh and my heart may fail, but God is the strength of my heart and my portion forever." (Psalm 73:26 ESV). I am striving to be the best that I can be. What would this world be if we all tried to do the same?

CHAPTER 4
Function at the Junction

For the Baby Boomers this song as one of our dance jams, the lyrics are iconic we would sing:

"I am getting ready for the function at the junction, and you better come on right now."

The song was written and performed by Shorty Long in the Sixties. I will give a new meaning to the young'uns from the elders. The functions of your bodies begin to slow at the junction (brain) if you do not pay attention or become conscience of the changes. Let me begin with flatulence or excess gas passing. So, let us get the farting humor out of the way so we can speak semi-intelligently regarding this normal bodily function. Benjamin Franklin wrote once "Fart Proudly" it was an essay about flatulence. Jack Nicholson said in the movie *Bucket List*, "never trust a fart" better to be sitting, than standing with poopy pants.

Young'uns, you can control the expelling process of gas retreat to a safer space without harming others or the air around you. With older folk, internal gas will get away from you and often without much warning. When in public, it is extremely difficult. I personally try to move away, or caution others when possible. Once in the grocery line after a conversation with some people a fart escaped without sound, the lady in the line let me know without biting her tongue how foul it was. I apologized that I had offended her and the air around us was indeed changed. My sister Brenda said she was standing in an aisle in a store when she let go. An employee, excited to help, started towards her. She attempted to deter the woman by saying she did not need help. The young lady continued walking towards her and became part of the unholy cloud that now hung over them both! Brenda said she thought to herself, "I tried to warn you!" The functions of our bodies change, the body redirects, or reclassifies functions to help us age and provide relief. It is so true that we are what King David said in the Bible "fearfully and wonderfully made" (Psalms 139:13-14). Bodily adjustments are made and must become accepted as part of the aging process.

The function is the attempt, the junction is the brain (control unit), and it is in control in executing bodily functions. Around fifty-five (others younger) when the clarity between function and the junction begin to cloud up. Case in point, if you wonder why older people seem to all speak at the same time, well, the process of the chain of thought (junction) and speaking the thought has an expiration date (seconds) this is at the function. My sisters and I have conversations and part of it is staying in the moment of the conversation or interaction. The result is occasionally the train of thought becomes lost. Can you imagine in the middle of a conversation you forget what you are talking about? Sometimes it comes back, other times gone forever! None the less there is a rhythm to it, you talk, while I forget, others talk, and I remember, interruptions (affects function) because the mind (junction) may again forget, got it? What I believe happens when there is a "brain fart", the person is not totally invested in the moment. The focus is lost because there is no FOCUS!

Remember we discussed slowing down, not being overly invested in multi-tasking. Slow down, I am learning when I am talking with my sisters to set aside the time, so that I can engage and be engaging. Pernitha and Brenda are my sisters, and ride or die the conversations we have, the time we spend together is "priceless." It is the same with my husband, daughters, grandson Princeton, family, and friends. Make it a point to be in the moments you share with others. The time we spend with them is a memory investment. Investing time in our conversations can benefit others.

A case to this point, after a long day of school and work (much younger), I came home to find my house filled with men watching tv and drinking.

After greeting them, I nonchalantly said, "a happy man is a working man" and went on my way.

Three weeks later, I was approached by one of these men, he said, "Thank you for saying a happy man is a working man." It was what he needed at the time to get him moving. He then said, "I am happy, as well as my family."

Those words became something in his life to consider, and he acted upon it. The reality was I was angry with them sitting in my home while I worked and continued my education. I said it to set their behinds on fire (to be mean), but it blessed someone. We can miss the intimacy of the moments in life that are blessings to ourselves or others. Young'uns, life is created in the moments we engage with others seeing life as a journey or each age a life chapter. Life is interaction, not a gilded cage or vacuum we live in, unless you are a recluse. Writing this was not created while I was alone, there were distractions, interaction, even aggravation, which created or sparked a thought. I am glad I am not alone, happy for the annoyances and interruptions from time to time.

It reminds me that I am still alive and able to accomplish purpose and live a life of faith that takes me from dawn to dusk.

CHAPTER 5
Philosophy of Aging

Philosophy is the study of a theoretical base of a particular branch of knowledge or *experiences*. The emphasis here is the experiences, we will delve into the knowledge of aging, some based on my experiences, others proven. Not everyone turns into the *fine wine* that is often used when speaking of beauty poetically; aging is not always pretty. What is important is the acceptance of aging we all will or can move through as best we can. Aging is the bodily functions changing. Sometimes it has felt like being in a ship without sails as if my mind were no longer in control of the new body, its new limits or direction. My body has a will of its own! Thank God that clinical medicine, psychology, and holistic approaches are in abundance there are choices to soothe the process. On the knowledgeable side, we can only hope to age mindfully with grace.

I come from the generation of the Baby Boomers, we invented multi-tasking and it is to our peril. According to statistics, Baby Boomers will rise from 1.2% in 2020 to 40.1% in 2050 that is equivalent to 10.3 million (alz.org 2015). A significant number worth noting will have the potential to suffer from dementia or Alzheimer's. Personally, my statement to these statistics, *but God*, (more regarding that later). As you start to age, your modus operandi (how you operate) changes. Start the process of slowing down tasking. This is not dumbing down, it is preservation in preparing for a long life. I have decided not to multi-task; rushing can ruin a day. Believers, the enemy (Satan) attempts to provoke us to hurry through life that can draw you into weariness. I am older, I just cannot rush my world. It is much too frustrating! My two sisters, my cousin, and I decide on a list of tasks for the day. We do not add to the list; we are true to the list. I personally allow myself three things to accomplish in a day using the following categories, house, events, and a personal day, a day I can do anything or nothing. Prayer is constant. Sunday belongs to God, that is for steadiness and spiritual rest. (Philippians 4:7)

Slowing down means also to be purposeful in the things you do. You should find a dedicated space for important things. Place them in a space that is visible. I found throwing or tossing things creates a mental block in recall memory. Placing them in a spot that is easily remembered. It is frustrating for me without both pairs of my reading glasses. I have found solutions for my keys (a hang bar) phone (a search app), but my glasses are still a mystery! Today, part of aging takes place in the mind, dementia, or Alzheimer's are two enemies of the aged. Do not frustrate yourself, it is natural to forget the mind is a computer that is vast.

Life expectancy for women has increased during the period of 1900 to 2000. White women 64.07% and black women 124.18%. The factors that affect these increases are lifestyle, physical and mental health, disease, and genetics (seniorliving.org 2022). Let me say to the mental diseases that affect aging, take a hike. No one wants you knocking on the door of our memories. You are an enemy that comes to steal, kill, and destroy. We do not want you around here! Hats off and respect for family members, caregivers, who care for those afflicted and researchers searching for cures.

For the elders, quiet your mind and slow down tasking. Young'uns, after consistent tasking, rest and clear your mind. Both elders and young'uns practice meditation, light candles, breathing exercises, be still, read a Bible verse (that relaxes me). Whatever it takes, slow it down! Taking time to close out your day without thinking of work, family, or tasks is necessary! In the morning, I have me-time when the house is quiet (everyone is asleep). It adds tranquility and the ability to cope with most things with calmness and thoughtfulness during the day. Just take some time for you.

It is *almost* impossible to multi-task as a senior. If you do, know there are consequences. In your flurry to get different things done you inevitability get things half done or not to accomplish the finished product you intended. An example, finding your glasses after three months in the dog's backpack under the bathroom sink, after ordering additional glasses, which are now also lost in the house! Hey, I slipped out my dentures in the car, put them in my jacket pocket, forgot, and took an hour to remember the location. Slow down and be thoughtful in your movements.

So, what is the word regarding the philosophy of aging? Avoid multitasking, put things away correctly while you have them consciously in your hand and on your mind (bears repeating). Do not rush to do anything. Stop and think about what you are attempting to do. The filter between my thoughts and my speech diminished noticeably as follows:

- Forties - I mulled my thoughts around a bit before I spoke

- Fifties - The filter from time to time was slipping
- Sixties - I retired, took my marbles and went home. Filter almost gone
- Seventies - Filter gone, "get out the way." (Not to the point of diminishing the soul of another, I am respectful).

The philosophy for my life is live, enjoy, acknowledging your purpose as often as possible, seek opportunities to do good. Strengthen your relationship with the Triune God (Father, Son, Holy Spirit) for guidance, share, and hang on to love. You hang on to love by allowing it to be the guiding star of your actions. A sizable portion of our lives is to serve others. By doing so we please God and we live a life of understanding that we are more than skin color, or a political party, or a country with a different world understanding. I am a believer who believes that we are more than a collection of differences, but a created being born into this world to create and share love while enjoying life. Yes, even the difficulties of it all. Every day is not perfect. Complexity, sorrow, and sadness have an end when I put my trust in the One that so loved, that He gave! (John 3:16)

Wisdom Arrested

CHAPTER 6
Wisdom Arrested

Wisdom arrested or seized means to become viable and useful to others and is an obtainable quest for elders. How do we obtain wisdom and live in our latter days with the mental capacity to reason with life events and physical health? Physical health is predicated on caring for ourselves as we age and staying actively moving. Our bodies were created for movement, it affects our mental state if we are unable to do so. I discovered having a relationship with God is lifesaving. Realizing that I have made mistakes, and some of those actions/mistakes are between myself and the Creator in a later discussion or book. Constant regret is a depression maker; some things we are unable to change. Personal growth is something we can thrive for; be easy on yourself, you can get to the desired state with patience. My mistakes taught me that without them, my learning curve narrows, and I am on a continuous treadmill of tiresome correction.

Wisdom is obtained after the mistakes. My mother was fond of saying, "Bought sense, is better than told sense." Meaning the mistakes you make is a wonderful way to deter you from making the same mistake again. If a person informs you that you made a mistake, you will ignore the warning and feel emboldened to do it your way! The mistake and its consequences are hopefully a learning experience! I made a plethora of mistakes. I then regrouped and tried to find a better way. This process brings wisdom. Scripture states that if any of you is deficient in wisdom, let him ask of [a]the giving God [Who gives] to everyone liberally *and* ungrudgingly, without reproaching *or* faultfinding, and it will be given him (James 1:5).

Our life journey is as a great teacher; learn to listen as often as you can to others, especially your elders (when they are in the mood to speak). You may learn, I certainly did! You do not grow old by being foolish. Hear all the sounds and sights that are around you pay attention to the inner voice that directs. I believe that when something is out of source there is an inner compass that beeps or sounds an alarm. I have come to know this as the *still small voice*. This world is so much more than what we see. I am indeed *spirit* there is a purpose on another level of knowing, understanding, and experiencing our world. The wisdom I have obtained has taught me to rely on the *still small voice*, not my intentions, but the nephesh spirit of God, breathed into the first Adam to become a *living soul* (knowing-mind – Genesis 2:7). Wisdom has instructed me that when I allow my flesh/mind to lust after *things* I seek without determining what is best for my life not weighing the alternatives, that can become a life journey altered.

You will understand when wisdom is arrested as part of your life, you will determine what it is for you and those things that are not. Wisdom you never talk, walk, or leave home without it! It is something ever present in the way you interact with others, how you manage challenges, your cognitive processes become thoughtful. It is more to life than self-satisfaction, our thoughts, our behavior, and our social and moral attitude can affect the many. We do not live on this rock (earth) alone. That is the essence of growing older, you settle into a purposeful self. You find yourself attempting to share life, wisdom, and purpose in creative ways. You become more of a motivational person who attempts to listen and encourage growth inwardly that accommodates others. I find myself enjoying the purposeful me instead of the impulsive me. My body and older self-enjoys contentment, expectations, and life's little surprises, I have this eagerness to regard others and using my time and wisdom as something to share.

This book was never meant to be about the pains of old, but the laughter and share the light and understanding of mental and physical aging and of our spiritual self. It is not a long writing on purpose, just a thoughtful glimpse to give a chuckle and provoke others to share their journey within their circle of influences or family. Family information and secrets kept is a deterrent for others to repeat over and over the same narrative. Generational curses are formed through secrets and the inability to share the historical mistakes that are made in a family. We all improve our situations by understanding what is difficult and those things that seem impossible. We all leg up by using our hands to lift others.

Scriptures inform me that I am an overcomer. For everyone born of God is victorious *and* overcomes the world; and this is the victory that has conquered *and* overcome the world—our [continuing, persistent] faith [in Jesus the Son of God] (John 5:4). If this little book does nothing but draw someone closer to family, smile at the history of one's life, and prepare the young for aging in some small way, then for me, it is purposeful and what matters to me.

CHAPTER 7
The Goals of the Aged Ones

As I have journeyed through life I would set goals, hoping that it would provide the lifestyle I was opting for, my beliefs, ethics, morals, are reflective in my interactions with others. The question for me became how to use the wisdom I have gained, is it possible for others to benefit from *my* wisdom? A Bible verse blessed me with insight. Forsake not [Wisdom], and she will keep, defend, *and* protect you; love her, and she will guide you. The beginning of Wisdom is to get Wisdom (skillful and godly Wisdom)! [For skillful *and* godly Wisdom is the principal thing], and with all you have gotten, get understanding (discernment, comprehension, and interpretation) (Proverbs 4:6-7**)**. Wisdom is a requirement of aging without it we wonder aimless through the rest of life an elder without a cause. Wisdom is instructive for me and others, it teaches us to be in the moment, not to hurry and hopefully give us the unction to be sensitive to others, not excluding their experiences, thoughts, or feelings that are vital to the gifting of wisdom. However, we must again be thoughtful and have understanding for those we interact. In my youth I enjoyed hearing and spending time with my elders. They had a way of interpreting and approaching situations in life with calmness and the choice to think of these times as acquired knowledge when led to share.

Wisdom is acquired, personal and complex, and associated with experience not always based in fact, but an understanding of life or experiences. Understanding is comprehension, insight, or good judgement into a situation. Another definition used in this discussion is intellect, the ability to reason abstractly and academically. As I become older, I recognize the need to navigate in a time that is futuristic in nature and that is owned by another generation. Cognitive patterns, development, life events are intense. The world is changing with consistency and for me it is at lightning speed. From my perspective, it was different when I was living my future. In my parent's time, technology was only in the beginning stages, manufacturing was king. Companies were created in my generation to create the "consumer life" or buy and satisfaction will come. The scripture in this chapter states that wisdom *will protect and watch over you*, wisdom is a gift we must learn to use wisely. The collection or buying of things does not ensure happiness, certainly we will not leave this physical realm and establish hierarchy on another plane. Wisdom must be spoken in love, it is the proverbial *pill* that should be swallowed easily to affect a life change, encourage a situation for the better, or provide options to insight. Scripture plainly states how we are to pass on wisdom to the next generation. "One generation shall praise thy works to another and shall declare thy mighty acts," (God) (Psalms 145:4). I believe that from generation to generation, we share our interactions with others, good or bad. That is called legacy. Everyone should ask the question, "What of myself am I leaving behind?" There is a poem I like by Meredith Malloy, "*I want to leave you something better than words or sound. Look for me in the people I have known or loved, if you cannot give me away, at least let me live on in your eyes.*"

As elders, we are to share our wisdom of life and characterize the experience in ways that will benefit others. Everyone has their own focus on how we get through life with as few bumps and bruises as possible. I have come to understand and recognized that living life with the knowledge of the Creator of all things guiding my life according to His purpose is learning Truth.

CHAPTER 8
Youth and Aging is Relative

I have been young and now am old, yet have I not seen the [uncompromisingly] righteous forsaken or their seed begging bread (Psalms 37:25).

How about this little tidbit, if you keep living you *will* prayerfully/hopefully become old! As I became older, I began to think about the life of my daughter without me, and how I can bless her. Part of my job is to encourage her. We talk about the eventuality of my death, how she is to manage the finances I leave behind, and how to honor my legacy. It is important to me to leave a monetary influence to help her upgrade her life. Yes, there is a biblical principal regarding this matter.

A good man leaves an inheritance [of moral stability and goodness] to his children's children, and the wealth of the sinner [finds its way eventually] into the hands of the righteous, for whom it was laid up (Proverbs 13:22).

I hope to also leave my baby wisdom for survival, the knowledge of God as her Source, and compassion to share the information with others. Young'uns, enjoy your youth, find your purpose, change jobs as many times as you want, which seem to be the order of the day. However, if you find a good partner, work with them. Remember why you made the decision that he or she was the *one*. Love is a decision, not something you fall into, as the movies suggest. I believe if you fall into love, you can easily fall out, and the effects are life consequential. If you can work together, come to a decision that benefits both your lives. Protect each other, love each other, and grow trying to stay together. Function as a unit, cleave to each other carry one another in the heart and keep God at the center of your life. Set goals and manage your lives together as *one*. Never go to sleep angry, it seems to polarize and intensify by the next day. Go to sleep with the understanding that a disagreement is not an anchor, but a difference in opinions. Be ready to forgive even when there is hurt or disappointment, work through it. Remember the qualities of love that formed the attraction. Allow mindfulness, compassion for others, kindness as a significant part of your modus operandi in your life journey. The relativity of youth and age, what you establish foundationally, will serve as anchors of survival when you grow older.

As you grow older, take into consideration those around you. You become a teacher as an elder or, at best, someone who knows a thing or two. God has been my steady or my foundation for guidance, how I live around and with others. I am not pushing God but sharing what has become *my* constant and what I believe will benefit all who are ready to understand Spirit. We come into this world unknowing. We should leave knowing well that we were created as image bearers. Why is love the most important of our existence and the center of all that is good around us? Why do we celebrate love with abandonment in everything we do or accomplish? Being so loved, (John 3:16) God created love and died in this earth for our purpose to live on this earth. Free will is a choice to do as we please. What I have discovered about *free will*, it comes with responsibility along with the possibility of outside influences that will deter purpose. To honestly believe that you are randomly born, live, and die serving self-purposes minimizes the complexity of life as if it is a stream that flows until it dries up! What I do between birth and death is relative to not only my life but the lives that I interact with. Cause and effect are an interaction of two things that make another thing happen. A man and women marry, a child is born, that child grows up, interacts, and shares with others and so on, and so forth! My youth and my elder self are purposeful and linked to the love of God and His image is the peace I live in these latter days; I surely hope that will be part of the legacy I leave behind.

CHAPTER 9
How Elders Cope

There is a saying among seniors, "You cannot grow old and be a *punk*." I prefer being called an elder instead of senior. It is a sign of respect. Also, it keeps me mindful of living in life moments and aware of the assignment at this point of what life truly requires. Bravery, a stiff upper lip, moxie, and stamina are necessary as your mind and body attempts to wreak havoc on your day to day. What I am witnessing among my peers and circle of influence is the evolution of the spirit. Being collectively aware of the physical and mental life changes in our world as an elder can be informative to the future of others as we witness and engage. There are elders who embrace the experience, others who feel the lightning speed of change as too *much* to cope and do not desire to engage. I thank God that I am experiencing these changes with women who find life

intriguing, my sister circle of women are true to themselves. Our pooled lessons are the foundation of shared experiences. When you are in the same boat, you do not feel alone or think that what is happening to your mind and body is singular. We all provide a life raft or anchor to surviving, we love each other, our grief is shared, we mourn with each other, and experience the love of God as foundational in our lives.

Your friends or circle of influence is not required to be large. However, it should be constant. My sisters Brenda, Pernitha, and Cousin Alice are my inner circle; we speak every day. My circle of influence is a group of twelve women ages eighty-six, the youngest fifty-two, friendships from sixty-seven years, the newest four months. These women are each important in my maintaining stability, and servility they keep me in check, and check me when I step out of character. This is part of my coping mechanism. I can also cope by not allowing stressful interactions or participation and minimize any frustration not by avoidance but by choice. I allow humor to guide me through, and thoughtfulness regarding life events which are natural occurrences of life. I listen intently and attempt to stay present and not allow my mind to wonder too far in the future. I cherish those things of the past that have kept me whole. I pray and make memories with those I love and who love me. I carry in my heart family and friends that exist in my heart and memory as blessed tokens. I am kind to those I chance to meet look for opportunities to do good to others, I try to be thoughtful in this personal adventure, eventful life, and thank God for keeping me healthy with the ability to comprehend and stay balanced cognitively.

Coping during my latter years is important, not allowing my experience to change or hinder my contributions by staying true to my purposes in life. I can hope and pray, young'uns, that this will help you find your coping tools. I am not perfect, there are faults. I do try to stay engaged and interact when it is purposeful, not to push an agenda. But I allow the Holy Spirit to direct me. I have learned to speak when it is appropriate, to not embolden myself in a situation if it is not warranted. My daughter cautions me regarding speaking to strangers. I do so only if I am led, which I can say these days are often. I am one who enjoys a person's smile even if it is a stranger. I would say I am gifted in trying to draw others to laughter!

My prayer, young'uns, is that you will find something in this chapter that you will tuck in your memory banks for later use. Speaking of memory banks, take it easy on the elders. Decades of stuff is stored in our brains, some easily accessible, other memory files may take a moment, or a day or two, to access. Trust me, I know from personal experiences. When this begins to happen, young'uns, do not become anxious. It is a natural progression of aging. When it begins happening, it may help, if you are feeling anxious, to involve your physician. They can run a few tests to assure you that everything is fine. The point, do not allow youself to be fearful. You need only to prepare, slow it down, do not multitask (worth repeating), and walk in purpose with thoughtfulness, mindfulness, and a love of life.

Time Behind, Time Ahead

CHAPTER 10
Time Behind the Time Ahead

I can look back but cannot go back. I can think of the mistakes I have made, the friends and time lost, but it all remains the same, unchanged. At this stage of my life, every day is a gift and a chance to participate in the world. I am aware, able to get around, can motivate myself, or as Ms. Fannie (Mom) would say, "Move under my own steam."

I made the decision at sixty-five to go back to school, get a degree, and received a bachelor of arts degree in Christian studies and a master's degree in mental health wellness with an emphasis on grief and bereavement. I had a 3.93 grade point average. This is not bucket list stuff, it is a commitment in life. I will use this knowledge to help my family and friends, or anyone who needs help in their grief journey. I am an advocate, as an elder who feels obligated to roll up my sleeves and use what I know to encourage or help others. I have more time behind me than in front of me but that is not a concern. Only to put one foot in front of the other, continue to discover in life, live my life chapters in peace, and share love. As an elder I understand that our life story is in our conversation, smiles, handshake, how we treat others, how we listen. My love language to others is giving, creating, sharing, teaching, not all lessons are pleasant, but always presented in love. Young'uns, your life is based in and on the decisions you make. Whether it is the next job, car, house, kids, clothing, the sums of life young'uns are based on our decisions. Please know that it has been the same for all generations, some things are unchanging. The lessons are part of the life journey to move us forward, to try and not hinder anyone, or for ourselves not to become stagnant. What matters or the difference that all should acknowledge or question, is *the decision* (purposeful) opposed to *a decision* (not contemplated) these are hard facts. Planning is essential when you are young, slow, and easy is much better than quick, and fleeting.

The time behind may have ended; however, it is a great launching pad for who we become. I am learning not to judge but to listen, hear the story, and find understanding for others as well as myself. Folks who are disrespectful or try to minimize the lives or difference in others and feel justified in doing so are hard for me to understand. It is time for that mentality to be eliminated, we should all pray for that! Life is a gift (old cliché). The time we use judging is better used in acceptance and or understanding. I practice daily not to judge. I do catch myself time to time judging, but I reel it in, start again, and renew the process.

Everyone who believes that life is about *I, you, them* (screams separatism) should practice thinking *me, you, us*. The way we think is indicative of who we are, and how we view and live our lives. It is my hope that I am reflective in life, trying to understand other cultures and traditions and to be respectful. I have come to know that I am a being created by a loving Creator, and I am to love others (agape – unconditional love, philia- friendship, fondness). This is not everyone's story, but it is what I have come to know, young'uns. I hope you all will come to know in your time. The time ahead is not spent wondering when I will check out of this physical world. It is spent living, thinking, sharing, interacting, experiencing as much peace and joy as I can find and give to others.

I have, however, prepared for the end of life. Life is not a staged act, it is reality. How we live counts towards how we experience the life around us that is important, one of those experiences is eventually *death* it happens to all. There I have said the word that is dreaded, ignored, and whisper about! Please take note, no one gets off this rock alive, and we should prepare, it is inevitable. I know there is more than the physical I see, and this decaying vessel where my spirit and soul is housed. There are over 2.2 billion believers who understand the same. I am fearfully and wonderfully made, His works are wonderful (Psalm 139:14). Ponder this, each person in this world shares physical similarities, hair, eyes, limbs, lungs, heart, and yet no one has the same fingerprint or DNA. Family shares familiar DNA, however, each can be uniquely identified to an individual. What do you think about that? Take your time and think about it, I will wait for the answer. Man evolving in knowledge, creativity, socially, okay, that is acceptable. However, the creation big bang theory uh, nope! The complexity of the created man is what I believe to be true according to scripture (Genesis 1:26-30). Man has yet to configurate the complexities of the body and still working in the dark, still there are mysteries and doctors refer to their offices still as *practices*. Here is another question, why do some survive diseases that take the life of another from cancer, heart disease, now in our memory banks, even the *pandemic*.

PREPARE YOURSELF young'un! Life is all about our taking our dreams and passions on our life journey, becoming purposeful, and operating in love. Be accepting, laugh, cry, share, talk, and walk out life, knowing that God has you in His hands. Elders, try to find a way to share what you have experienced with family, friends, or anyone who will listen. Have patience with the young'uns, sometimes their heads are not in the same space as yours. Just plant a thought or seed that can take root and grow!

In conclusion of my sharing in this little book, I hope that the elders will find things that are comparable and some laughter. For the young'uns, my prayer is that wisdom is found, understanding is received, and that some of the lessons I passed are helpful and used. I have a prayer for myself. I hope that some of you will stand in prayer of agreement with me, all that read this book. Prayerfully, my hope is God will continue to allow me to use my gifts to share more of this life with everyone. I love life, I enjoy my days on this earth, and I pray that transition will be easy and what I left behind will be useful. I believe in my soul that absence from the body is truly being in the presence of the Creator (2 Corinthians 5:8).

Thank you!

LANGUAGE GUIDE OF THE ELDERS

Each generation has its own language or slang that is universal to their peers. Some of that language is traditional, culturally specific to a region, or it can be global. Elders are no different, communication is often historical or generational. The purpose of this portion of the book is to share that "lingo" in hopes some of it is maintained, remembered, or passed on. Just maybe this will be a reminder of a perhaps a grandparent or family member and spark a memory or two. I have picked up some of the language today such as being *on "fleek"* meaning fashionable, or a party or an event is *"lit"*. I wish that I had an opportunity to be a "GOAT", the *greatest of all time*. There is still time! I feel that most of my life I have kept things *100*! My absolute favorite of this generation is *"woke,"* meaning to be socially, politically, ethically, and morally *awake*. If this becomes the outcry of many, there is hope for this world that we live in. It is an indication that the world will be kinder, more understanding, accepting, aware, and more respectful of everyone and everything around them. This slang, I hope young'uns, becomes your outcry and purpose! Now let's investigate the language the elders used.

ELDER SLANG

Slang	Meaning
Fair to Middling	Feeling good/average
Cracking on someone	Making fun of situation/someone
Give me my pocketbook	When it is a purse!
Tennis shoes	Really sneakers
Tin foil	Aluminum
Busting moves	Dancing
Cook	Doing something good.
Soda water/soda pop	Pepsi, Coke
Jaw jerkin'	Excessively talking too much.
Get down	Anything done well.
Faded	Under the influence.
Later gator	Cool way of saying goodbye.
It is what it is.	Done deal.

That's the way the
cookie crumbles.
Forget about it.
That's BOSS
Out of sight
Sock it to me
Boom, there it is.
Let me hip you.

You molded.

Things happen.
Not a problem.
Surprisingly good.
Stupendous, good
Give it to me straight.
This is the deal.
Provide you with
information.
You should be ashamed.

SCRIPTURE REFERENCES
For Elders (Scriptures to Encourage)

Isaiah 46:4

Even to old age I am he, and even to gray hairs I will carry you. I have made, and I will bear. Yes, I will carry, and will deliver.

Deuteronomy 34:7

Moses was one hundred twenty years old when he died. His eye was not dim, nor his strength gone.

Isaiah 40:31

But those who wait for Yahweh will renew their strength. They will mount up with wings like eagles. They will run, and not be weary. They will walk, and not faint.

2 Corinthians 4:16

Therefore, we don't faith, but though our outward man is decaying, yet our inward man is renewed day by day.

Acts 20:28

Take heed, therefore to yourselves, and to all the flock, in which the Holy Spirit has made you overseers, to shepherd the assembly of the Lord and God which he purchased with his own blood.

1 Timothy 5:17

Let the elders who rule well be counted worthy of double honor, especially those who labor in the word and in teaching.

Hebrews 1:14

Aren't they all serving spirits sent out to do service for the sake of those who will inherit salvation?

Romans 8:35, 38, 39

Who shall separate us from the love of Christ" Could oppression, or anguish, or persecution, or famine, or nakedness, or peril, or sword? For I am persuaded that neither death, nor life, nor angels, nor principalities, nor things present, nor things to come, nor powers, nor height, nor depth, nor any other created thing will be able to separate us from God's love which is in Christ Jesus our Lord.

Philippians 4:6
In nothing be anxious, but in everything, by prayer and petition with thanksgiving, let your requests be made to God.

SCRIPTURE REFERENCES
For the Young'uns

Leviticus 19:32

You shall rise up before the gray head and honor the face of the elderly; and you shall fear (reverence) our God.

Deuteronomy 32:6

Remember the days of old. Consider the years of many generations. Ask your father, and he will show you; your elders, and they will tell you.

Matthew 6:33

But seek first God's Kingdom, and his righteousness; and all these things will be given to you as well.

2 Timothy 1:7

For God didn't give us a spirit of fear, but of power, love, and self-control.

Romans 9:12

Let love be without hypocrisy. Abhor that which is evil. Cling to that which is good. In love of the brothers be tenderly affectionate to one another; in honor preferring one another; not lagging in diligence; fervent in spirit; serving the Lord; rejoicing in hope; enduring in troubles; continuing steadfastly in prayer.

Galatians 5:22-23

But the fruit of the Spirit is love, joy, peace, patience, kindness, goodness, faith, gentleness, and self-control. Against such things there is no law.

Psalms 118:24

This is the day that Yahweh has made. We will rejoice and be glad in it.

Proverbs 15:18

A wrathful man stirs up contention, but one who is slow to anger appeases strife.

Proverbs 14:29

He who is slow to anger has great understanding, but he who has a quick temper displays folly.

I Corinthians 13:4-7

Love is patient and is kind. Love doesn't envy. Love doesn't brad, it is not proud, doesn't seek its own way, is not provoked, takes no account of evil; doesn't rejoice in unrighteousness, but rejoices with the truth; bears all things, believes all things, hopes all things, and endures all things.

REFERENCES

www.seniorliving.org/history/1900-2000-changes-life-expectancy-united-states/

*Michelle Obama American attorney, author, mother First Lady of the United States 2009-2017

All Scripture sare quoted from the Amplified Bible translation unless otherwise noted.

ACKNOWLEDGEMENTS

Art by Pernitha Hearne

Brenda Stephens Book Production Overseer

Ideas and Critiques

Lavada Celestine

Kina Stephens

Elizabeth Faine

Annette Williams

Shirley's influences!

GOD, *my inner circle* Pernitha Hearne, Brenda La Faye Stephens, Alice Davis.

My Circle

Shirleyne Bates

Eleanor Bowden

Vivian Brooks

Emma Davis

Lavada Celestine

Edna Clarke

Latanya Lee

Luberta Reed

Jessie Mae Rhone

Vivian Thompson

Rosa Wayne

Annette Williams

Spirit Counselors

Pastor Joe B. Smith, Jr, Ph.D.

Pastor Keith Garrett Ph.D.

Pastor Jeff Moore

The late Bishop Kenneth L. Green, Sr. Ph.D.

Spirit 1's

Pastor Annette Vance

Carolyn Johnson

ABOUT THE AUTHOR

Shirley Hearne-Clark is seventy-two years old, a native of Los Angeles, California living in Hemet, California. *Love letter to the Young'uns* is her first book. She lives with her husband Camille Clark, mother-in-law Emelienne Clark, (a *centurion* at one hundred years old), daughter Enijua J. Williams, and fur babies Jaxx, Toto, and Popcorn the cat. She has one grandson Princeton, whom she adores. Shirley is an ordained minister and loves to sing, write, and read. She believes God for her life, and family is important always. She believes that the Bible is the word of God the answer for our lives and understands that all of humanity should be linked together in unity and love globally! She received both a bachelor's and master's degree from Grand Canyon University. Her favorite Bible verse is, "Trust in Yahweh with all your heart, and don't lean on your own understanding. In all your ways acknowledge him, and he will make your path straight." (Proverbs 3:6-7). Shirley is one of the hosts of a podcast with her two sisters called Elders *N* Sync. This is a J & F girls and *cousin* endeavor.